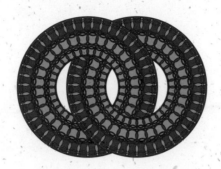

THE SILENCE OF MEN

THE SILENCE OF MEN

poems by Richard Jeffrey Newman

CavanKerry ◈ Press LTD.

Library of Congress Cataloging-in-Publication Data

Newman, Richard Jeffrey, 1962-
The silence of men : poems / Richard Jeffrey Newman.-- 1st ed.
p. cm.
ISBN-13: 978-0-9723045-8-0
ISBN-10: 0-9723045-8-4
I. Title.

PS3614.E65S55 2006
813'.54--dc22

2005027470

Author photograph by BeechTree Images © 2005
Cover art: "Silence of Men" Peter Cusack © 2005
Cover and book design by Peter Cusack

CavanKerry Press Ltd.
Fort Lee, New Jersey
www.cavankerrypress.org

First Edition 2006
Printed in the United States of America

NEW ✧ VOICES

CavanKerry Press is dedicated to springboarding the careers of previously unpublished poets by bringing to print two to three New Voices annually. Manuscripts are selected from open submission; CavanKerry Press does not conduct competitions or charge reading fees.

Awarded a Citation of Excellence from the New Jersey State Council on the Arts, CavanKerry Press is grateful for the support it receives from the Council.

Acknowledgments

"You Will, Of Course, Assume It Is For You" and an earlier version of "Kashrut" appeared in *Prairie Schooner*. In addition, "Kashrut" was featured on the web site "Poetry Daily."

"Isaac's Story" and "Between Men" appeared in *Another Chicago Magazine*.

"The Silence of Men," "Commerce" and "What I Carry With Me" have appeared in *The Pedestal Magazine*, (www.thepedestalmagazine.com).

"Wormholes" and "Dear Yoon" appeared in the *Birmingham Poetry Review*.

Earlier versions of "Sarah's Story," "Rachel's Story," and "Ezra's Story" appeared in *Beyond Lament: Poets Of The World Bearing Witness to the Holocaust* (Northwestern University Press) as sonnets number 25, 30 and 33 respectively.

"Ibrahim's Story" appeared in *Out of Line*.

"Covenant" appeared in *The Potomac Review*.

"The Speed and Weight of Justice" appears in *Access Literature*, Wadworth Publishers in Summer 2005.

"Who Knew?" and "After The Funeral" appeared in *Helix*.

"Because," "Mirage," and "Light" appear in *New Works Review*, (www.newworks.com).

"My Father Loses His Grip" appeared in *Xanadu*.

"Dear Ji-in" appeared in *Paper Street Press*.

For Adrienne,
who believed in my writing
almost before I did.

And for Maryam and Shahob,
my new seasons.

Contents

Foreword

If beauty resides in truth, then there are moments of severe beauty and tantalizing energy in Richard Jeffrey Newman's, *The Silence Of Men*. Beginning with the collection's title, one is keenly aware of a provocative tension, and the mind makes a few questions stand up in the heart. The poet has our attention. Why a silence of men? Does this silence exist between fathers and sons, brothers, or between most men and women? Is it natural or unnatural? In this sense, the title works as an axiom that creates a motion.

The reader's inquisitive journey begins with the first seventeen lines of "What I Carry With Me":

> I came home that night,
> > my shirt thick with the
> > > smell of your cigarettes,
>
> to a sleeping wife and child,
> > and I sat in the large green chair
> > > at the other end of the house,
>
> and I stared in disbelief and sorrow:
> > I no longer loved you.
> > > The living room walls,
>
> lit up briefly by the headlights
> > of a passing car, recalled to me
> > > the first bedroom where I woke
>
> crying from nightmares
> > you saved me from, your palm
> > > against my cheek, your lips
>
> pressed to my forehead, amulets
> > I took back with me to sleep.

Here, truth is discovered in the poem's straightforward tone, in its coloration, without facade or extreme embellishment. No, this isn't a confession exacted by a grand inquisitor, but it is a voice we can trust, and even believe in. And, yes, this is the primary triumph of *The Silence of Men*. We have been taught to equate silence with strength—the strong, silent type.

Oftentimes, we are silent about what we witness. But Richard Newman's narrator suggests that there's inherent strength in the telling and sharing, in a dialogue. His poetry dares us, as men, as human beings, to share what we have experienced and imagined—the good and the bad. He seems to be saying that dialogue is what makes each of us whole. Not in a gush, but through a measured language that embraces art. Also, the speaker in this collection suggests that we are responsible for what we know, for what we've witnessed and dreamt, and for what we don't say to ourselves and each other.

The speaker in *The Silence of Men* is determined to gain a sense of Self. And, at times, as the reader journeys through this collection, he or she may feel that the narrator is speaking to himself or having a dialogue with some phantom other, but what always comes through is a reflection that almost approaches a moment of redemption. Though there are numerous stories here that reflect the past, we remain in the urgency of the present, fully engaged and compassionate.

In this chronicle of confrontations, this journey, everything culminates in a five-line poem entitled "Catching My Breath":

> My body has learned many lies,
> but here, in this bed we share,
> they fall from me till I am clean,
> a tree in winter,
> awaiting the new season.

Of course, this "new season" can only happen through an act of self-forgiveness, after silence has been bridged and a dialogue has been created. *The Silence of Men* is daring: there's a moral gesture at the heart of this collection, but the poetry isn't moralistic or didactic. In fact, when the narrator says, "I'm not being hard on myself," we know that the whole journey has been about freedom, renewal, and release.

—*Yusef Komunyakaa*

Princeton NJ

Watching a pair of swans in this small bay off the ocean.
You at the water's edge like a kid blowing bubbles.
Sun at my back, the disappointment of no mail, of yesterday's rejection.
Across the water, on the other side of a small finger of land, a sail.

I provide the boat beneath it.

—Richard Jeffrey Newman

THE SILENCE OF MEN

What I Carry With Me

I came home that night,
    my shirt thick with the
        smell of your cigarettes,

to a sleeping wife and child,
    and I sat in the large green chair
        at the other end of the house,

and I stared in disbelief and sorrow:
    I no longer loved you.
        The living room walls,

lit up briefly by the headlights
    of a passing car, recalled to me
        the first bedroom where I woke

crying from nightmares
    you saved me from, your palm
        against my cheek, your lips

pressed to my forehead, amulets
    I took back with me to sleep.
        These days, I secure what I can—

doors, windows, a careful glance
    up and down the street, or a person,
        or the car parked on our block

too long in one spot—but as often
    as not, the phantom I fear
        wears the face you showed me

while we ate our prime ribs
    cooked medium rare,
        and drank our drinks,

vodka and beer, and argued
    about terror and self-preservation,
        and—you insisted it must be named—

the point where love of who you are
    and love of where you are
        become the same love.

I wanted to ask you
    how it could be otherwise,
        but you were as alien to me

in that restaurant's darkened corner
    as all the languages I don't speak,
        as the foreigners you railed against

are suspicious to you. Did you hear
    the woman entertaining friends behind us
        with stories of *fucked-up A-rabs*

and *Islamic bloodlust?* She laughed,
    cheered the bombing promised
        by the man who leads our nation,

and her friends laughed with her,
    and they clinked their glasses,
        and I am ashamed—ashamed!—

that I didn't interrupt
    whichever one of us needed interruption
        to tell those women to shut the hell up.

Which I should've told you as well.

Which also shames me.

As a boy, I loved you
    the way I learned to talk,
        because, like words, you

were what I had to work with,
    but then you left, and left again,
        and I wish I could say

it wasn't you I rode away from
    in the cab with the Sikh driver
        who, from the moment I closed the door

on the hopeful farewell you called out—
    Say hi for me!—wouldn't stop talking
        about the never-changing Muslims

who murder his people
    and want to rule the world:
        What they started, you know—he turned

with his hands on the wheel to face me
    as we inched up First Avenue, smiling
        like I too wore a turban—*you know,*

what they started in Punjab,
    they continue in Kashmir. But it was
        you I saw standing in the street

as the rain began to fall,
    and it was you I spoke to
        as the taxi turned west

on Fifty Seventh Street, *My wife*
    is Muslim. Do you think
        I'm in danger? We rode

the rest of the way in silence,
    and because I could imagine
        surviving deaths that transformed me

into him, I tipped the driver anyway,
    and he said *thank you,*
        and I wished him peace.

The click of my heels
    bounced and multiplied
        off the walls on either side

of the deserted street I took
    instead of the subway home.
        I stepped, without breaking stride

or conversation—I was still
    talking to the you in my head—
        past three sleeping men, the one

on the left snoring
    flat on his back, his pants,
        beltless, zipperless, bunched

nearly halfway down his thighs.
    His penis, a dark flagpole
        swaying in the wind of his dreams,

pointed back over his eyes
    to the newsprint red-white-and-blue
        and the dead-or-alive front page

he and his buddies had taped
    to the storefront window
        that was their headboard.

As I stood there thinking,
    What else do they have? an image
        resolved into clarity

of the escargot you wouldn't name
    till I put it on my tongue,
        and I was thirteen, and I tasted it,

and the flavor unfolded in me—
    garlic and butter and wine—
        and I opened to its foreignness

as I've been opening ever since,
    and so what I have
        is my son's voice

calling out that night, *Boro!*
    Boro kenar!—Get away from me!—
        in a nightmare he'd say

the next morning
    was invaded by white trees
        he couldn't kill,

and what I have
    is the shadow of my wife's body
        against darkness, running to him

as if his life, or hers, hung
    waiting to begin or end,
        and what I have

is this weight that's made itself at home
between my lungs: the heaviness
of leaving you behind.

October 16–November 16, 2001,

during the bombing of Afghanistan at the

start of George W. Bush's "War on Terrorism"

Like Wet Clay On A Wheel

She leaned into his hands and he took her,
kneading her back on the bench next to mine
in the weekend chaos of Washington
Square Park, where I sat trying to let go
of what I couldn't help but hold; and when
his touch pulled her gaze up out of herself
and chance turned it towards mine, I saw
in her eyes how much I wanted to be
beneath hands like his, that knew which muscle
held my tears, and how much pressure would be
permission to let them go. Today, I woke
for the first time since we buried him
wanting my brother alive: someone to tell
I've made it this far, who won't ask *From where?*

Again

The front door opens onto the hallway
running through the apartment like a spine.
To the left, the living room, the green couch
there's somewhere a picture of me kissing
cousin Deborah on, and the bridge table
where Grandma Ruth taught us to play Mah Jong.
Further down, the kitchen, the brown chairs,
my father and his father drinking beer,
talking the horses. Straight ahead, the door
I don't remember ever seeing open.

He says he's going to teach me a lesson.
He says it's my mother's fault. He pushes me
back into the bathroom. Then nothing but my
father sleeping. The dream ends. I've wet my bed.

Rachel's Story

After each transport was gassed, we'd remove
gold teeth and fillings and peel off the skin,
especially from young ones that had been
tattooed. What was left we took to the grave
that never seemed to fill. I didn't grieve
till bodies that had been my daughter and son
passed before me. I let them pass and when
the guard walked by asked him to shoot me. His laugh
is with me still, *And who gave you the right*
to say when you will die? Or are you god?
If I'd thrown myself into the pit
or fallen to the floor, I'd now be dead.
The Nazi laughed again and turned away.
I'd chosen life. Or had it chosen me?

Working The Dotted Line

I don't remember what vacation
I was home for, or how Beth
managed to be in New York
on the one day we'd have
the apartment to ourselves,
but I think I recall
my mother's hanging crystals
scattering the afternoon sunlight
in small rainbows that shimmied
on the walls and on our skin,
and I can still see Beth stretching
nervous along the length
of the daybed's mattress,
and my fingers tracing
the ridges of her ribs
as she tugged at my erection.
I'm ready. Let's do it!

It was her first time, not mine,
but it was my first condom,
and I'd forgotten to read the directions,
so I stood there growing soft,
squinting at the print on the box
telling me the step-by-step
I needed to learn
was on the inside.
I ripped the cardboard open
and sat reading on the bed's edge,
thumbing the foil-packed
lubricated circle,
trying to visualize
what I had to do.

Beth reached into my lap
to ready me again,
but when I tore along the dotted line,
our protection, like a goldfish
taken by hand from its bowl,
slipped from my grasp
and landed under the desk
my mother sat at
when she paid the bills.
When I picked it up,
it was covered with the dust
and small particles of dirt
that settle daily into all our lives,
so I didn't put the next one on
till I was kneeling hard
between Beth's open legs.
She raised herself on her elbows,
smiling that the second skin
we needed to keep us safe
should make me so clumsy,
but once I let go
of what the instructions called
the *reservoir tip*—I thought
of the dams holding water back
in the mountains near where she lived
and what would happen if they broke—
her smile disappeared
and bunching the sheet beneath her
into her fists, she lifted
her butt onto the pillow
we'd heard would make things easier.

I bent for a quick look
at where I had to go
and climbed up onto her,
trying with one hand

to be graceful and accurate
and with the other
to balance over her
without falling.
At her first grimace
I pulled back. *No!*
She shook her head, eyes
clamped shut and then
staring wide, her voice
a whisper through clenched teeth,
Just do it! Get it over with!

So I entered her again, trying
from the tightness in her face
to gauge how hard not to push,
but when she cried out anyway,
I left her body one more time
and crouched over her,
my latex-covered penis
nosing downward
towards her navel,
and I placed my palms
against her cheeks,
I cannot hurt you like this!

Look, it's going to hurt, she said.
There's no other way.
And I've chosen you!

And since I wanted so much to be her choice,
I kissed her eyelids and her mouth,
and with my eyes buried
in the hollow of her neck
moved slowly in
till I felt her flesh
stop giving way. Then,

with one arm around her rib cage
and the other around her head,
holding her tight against my chest,
I pulled down and thrust up
in a single motion I breathed through
like I was lifting heavy boxes.
She screamed into the muscle
just above my collar bone,
bit deep into my flesh,
and, as she bled onto me,
I bled.

We said nothing afterwards.
We didn't cuddle
or smile at each other as we dressed
or walk hand in hand
to the train that took her home;
and I did not ask her
what her silence meant,
nor she mine, but if she had,
I would've told her this:
My wordlessness was shame.
I'd no idea how not to hurt her;
and I would've told her
I wanted it to do over,

which is what I'd tell her even now.

The Taste Of A Little Boy's Trust

Snow still falling this late,
when each house framed
by the window above my desk

is dark, and even my wife's breathing
has grown indistinguishable
from the quiet, snow still falling

as a truck rolls by, big-cat-svelte
on eighteen wheels, orange
running lights spreading

up and down my block
a Halloween glow
in mid-December,

like a space vessel landing,
bringing me the boy I was
standing in the courtyard, searching

the descending whiteness
for the shapes of ships
I longed to fly away on,

snow still falling this late
when I could be sleeping,
the way I should have been

the night I saw my mother nude,
and her friend on his back, and them both
too slow to hide what they were doing,

and I told my brother and we tried it,
and we tried to understand
why grown-ups did it—*how could you let someone*

pee in your mouth?—snow still falling this late
is the whisper we tried to laugh in, breath
the old man dropped, syllable—

when—by syllable—*will I*
see you?—into my ear, and I
couldn't move, wouldn't,

and so it wasn't me
who followed him upstairs, who listened
to the lock click shut in the door, and it wasn't me

whose belt he unbuckled, and when
his pants joined mine on the floor, it wasn't
me he pled with, whose head he used

both hands to pull towards him
when I balked, whose mind
at this moment always whites out

until it wasn't me
who unlocked the door and walked
to where the snow is still falling,

as if even now he waited
in the apartment above mine,
and no matter how many times

my brother asks, I won't go out,
not even to be first sled down
a virgin hill of the season's new snow.

Going Somewhere Else

Suggesting trees, a voice floats.
The boy is looking. Over
his shoulder, we see the road

run past a barbed wire fence,
but language I put between
his lips turns his thoughts to the

river, and we turn with him.
A cymbal crash places rocks
he climbs down to just inside

the line where shadow becomes
sunlight. Still playing, the man
with the flute rises, gestures

for the others to follow.
At the back of the theater,
hooded figures lock the doors.

A sudden blue-green spotlight
focused stage left. Time has passed.
Books fall from the sky, snowflakes

the young man catches on his
tongue, and he his smiling,
but the woman whose rhythms

fill the melody's empty
spaces lifts her hands: Nothing
driving the song now but the

need each note creates in us
for the next one, and the next,
till the orchestra fades and,

center stage, I sit alone,
sketching at this piano
the hills I once imagined

walking with you, twilight hills
at once familiar and strange,
as from the top of the Pentlands

Edinburgh is all cities
and one city. Hills where my
companions—themselves composed

partly of parts of me—are
unaware, that with these notes
they do not hear, on these keys

that are not mine, I give them
lives they have never lived.

Edinburgh University, 1985—Jackson Heights,
NY, 1998

Light

In the dream, my life was smoke: I couldn't breathe.
So I ran, unwrapping myself down the beach
till your skin, the ocean, lapped at my knees.
I dove in. Your voice was a current,
a melody gathering words to itself
for us to sing, and we sang them,
and they swirled around us, iridescent fish
bringing light to the world you were for me;

and then I was water, a river
washing the night from your flesh,
and I cradled your body rising in me
till you were clean, glowing,
and when you surfaced, glistening,
there was not an inch of you I didn't cling to.

Wormholes

*Wormhole: In physics, a hypothetical connection
between widely separated regions of space-time.*

It's afternoon, hours before he needs to be awake,
but he has to tell me: My friends are waiting,
and my mother isn't home. I'm seven.

He's her second husband, drives a night truck
delivering bread we get free loaves of. My tears—
his midday sleep is holy ground—

start the moment I call him.
On the other side, he's above me,
his fists and his voice a jackhammer's rage.

Another hole opens and my hair
is in the hand he drags me
to the kitchen with, still yelling, pushing

ice against the blood across my face.
Then I'm wrapped in a blanket, sitting
beside my mother in their bedroom.

Why does he always call me sissy?
Stop crying, she answers. *You fell*
out of bed. That's all.

Who Knew?

I'm waiting for the tears that didn't come
when they put him in the ground, that wouldn't come
among the family friends and relatives
who later came to mourn. The small talk
they made of other deaths to make their own
smallness less apparent made my brother's dying
smaller by the hour. One woman,
lost in a cousin's cancer, turned to me
as someone handy to do what her grief
would not allow her to do, *Richard, sweetie,*
be a dear, bring me an ashtray. After lunch,
I recited kaddish. The same woman
took my arm, *That was wonderful!*
Who knew you had such Jewish in you?

Slice Of Life

Bleeker Street, Carpo's Café, the couple
next to me speaking French inside the song
the flamenco guitarist I could touch if I wanted to
is weaving around the waitress I can't stop

holding up to the light in the narrow crib
of my seven-and-a-half pyong
Chamshil apartment, where the woman
whose twin she could be still curls

naked in my arms, and I believe each word
she whispers against my losing her. That weekend
at the ski resort north of Seoul, when she told
her husband on the phone

she'd come alone so she could think,
I was still quivering inside her,
licking the sweat from her neck,
feeding on what she offered me,

fire-warmed against the snow,
the way I'm feeding now,
holding each spoonful in my mouth
till the flavor dissipates, not dipping again

into Carpo's famous homemade black bean soup
until my tongue feels neither hot nor cold.
When I'm done, I leave—as eventually I left her—
for home, where my key sticks in the front door,

and in the mailbox. In the elevator,
I open the first letter: *They tied this Turkish girl*

to a cross and left her hanging.
Then they cut away her clothes and did the rest

with gun barrels and a broken broomstick....
Any size donation is welcome, but may we suggest
thirty-five dollars? Hours later, the pull of sleep
a weak tug on what troubles me, I sit in bed

and try to give the dream a shape this page will hold:
They hung me by my wrists. Each time I said
I didn't know, they beat me with a bat, waving knives
they vowed would slice my Jewish dick in half.

Years before, in my waking life, they chased me
with stones big as baseballs, pinning me down
behind the wide oak tree across from the Lutheran church.
Fucking Heeb! Ya' lucked out this time!

A cop drove slowly by but didn't stop.
I stayed put until I caught my breath.

Seoul, 1989–Jackson Heights, 2002

Ibrahim's Story

I always buy candles when I invite
someone for supper. They remind me of
Erev Shabbat dinners I used to have
in the years before there was a Jewish State
with the families of my Jewish friends. Rafat,
village of my birth, is gone. Now I live
in Bethlehem, in exile, and weave
carpets, and write songs, and watch, and wait.

Once, sitting among stones on this land
we all call home, an American guide
told a teen tour group from the States that trees
my ancient namesake planted moved the breeze
around them, *roots nourished by Jewish blood.*
Like yours, I thought, moving on, gun in hand.

Then, As Now, I Couldn't Look Away

I step in front of my building over
rats my fellow tenants killed this morning.
Joking to myself that maybe people
eat them here, that I, without knowing it,
might already have, I find one half-alive,
a hole poked through its stomach, and I'm back
in Dutchess County watching grandpa
in the kitchen doorframe
brace the rifle against his shoulder,
take aim and, sometimes,
kill what nested
beneath the field's far corner. Once,
before they could catch me,
I ran to where the bullet flew and found,
laying on its side, a woodchuck still breathing,
shaking back and forth, like the men who davened
Shabbes morning in shul. I stood transfixed,
watching the animal's dying
gather strength, wondering
which struggling breath
would be its last.

Seoul, May 1989

Coitus Interruptus

Naked at the window, my wife calls me
as if someone is dying, and someone
almost is, pinned to the concrete face down
beneath the fists and feet and knees of three

policemen. I'm still hard from before she
jumped out of bed to answer the question
I was willing not to ask when the siren
stopped on our block, but now I'm here, and I see

the man is Black, and how can I not
bear witness? They've cuffed him,
but the uniforms continue to crowd our street,
and the blue-and-whites keep coming,

as if called to war, as if the lives
in all these darkened homes
were truly at stake, and that's the thing—
who can tell from up here?—maybe

we're watching our salvation
without knowing it. Above our heads,
a voice calls out *Fucking pigs!*
but the ones who didn't drag the man

into a waiting car and drive off
refuse the bait. They talk quietly,
gathered beneath the streetlamp
in the pale circle of light

the man was beaten in, and then
a word we cannot hear is given
and the cops wave each other back
to their vehicles, the flash and sparkle

of their driving off
throwing onto the wall of our room
a shadow of the embrace
my wife and I have been clinging to.

When I was sixteen, Tommy
brought to my room before he left
the Simon and Garfunkel tape
I'd put the previous night

back among his things. He placed it
on the bookshelf near the door
he'd slammed shut two days earlier
when he was holding a butcher's cleaver

to my mother's life. I wanted
to run after him and smash it at his feet;
I wanted to grab him by the scruff of the neck
and crush it in his face, to dangle him

over the side of our building with one
ankle in my left hand and the *Greatest Hits*
in my right and ask him
which I should let drop.

But I didn't, couldn't really:
he was much too big,
and I was not a fighter,
and one of my best friends right now

lives with her son in the house
where her husband has already hit her
with a cast iron frying pan,
and so there is no reason to believe

she is not at this moment cringing
bruised and bleeding in a corner
of their bedroom, or that she is not,
with her boy and nothing else in her arms,

running the way my mother
didn't have a chance to run,
and there's nothing I can do
but look at the clock—Sunday,

11:11 PM—and remind myself
it's too late to call, that my calls
have caused trouble for her already.
When they pushed Tommy in handcuffs

out the front door, past where my mother sat,
quiet, unmoving, and I did not know
from where inside my own rage and terror
to pull the comfort I should have offered her,

the officer making sure Tommy
didn't trip or run winked at me, smiling
as if what had happened were suddenly
a secret between us, and this our signal

that everything was okay. I wondered
if his had been the voice, calm
and deep with male authority—*Son,
are you sure your mother's in there*

against her will?—that when I called
forced me to find the more-than-yes
I can't remember the words to
that convinced the cops they had to come.

2.

Sophomore year, walking the road
girdling the campus. Up ahead, a woman's voice
pleading with a man's shouting to stop.
A car door slamming, engine revving,

and then wheels digging hard into driveway dirt
that when I got there was a dust cloud
obscuring the blue vehicle's rear plate.
The woman sprawled on the asphalt,

her black dress spread around her
like an open portal her upper body
emerged from. She pulled
the cloth away from her feet,

which were bleeding, and I drove
to where her spaghetti strap sandals
lay torn and twisted beyond repair.
She left them there. Then to her home,

two rooms in a neighborhood house,
and I helped her onto the bed
that was her only furniture, and filled
a warm-water basin to soak her feet,

and he had not hit her, so there was nothing
to report, but she said she was afraid
and would I sit with her a while.
We talked about her home in Seoul,

the man her parents picked for her
that she ran to America to avoid marrying,
and here she laughed—first trickle
of spring water down a winter mountain—

So instead I take from Egypt! I so stupid!
Then: *What you think? Can man and woman*
sleep same bed without sex? I said yes.
So, please, tonight, you stay here? Maybe he coming back.

He fear white American like you. I was not a fighter,
but I stayed, and in the morning when I left,
she said *kamsahamnida*—thank you—
and she bowed low, and she did not

ask my name, nor I hers, and though
I sometimes looked for her on campus,
I never saw her again. Just like Tommy,
whom I forgot to say before was white.

Just like the Black woman who lived downstairs
before I got married, whose cries—*Help!*
Please! He's killing me!—and the dead thud
of him, also Black, throwing her

against the wall, and his screaming—
Shut up, bitch! Fucking whore!—filled the space
till I was drowning. The desk sergeant
didn't ask if I knew beyond a doubt

that she was being beaten,
but when she opened her front door
to the two men he sent, she shrieked
the way women shriek

in bad horror movies
when they know they're going to die,
and I almost felt sorry for calling.
A few weeks later,

a voice on the phone: *You know*
what's going on below you, right?
Please, tape a message to the door: "Mr. Peters
has been trying to reach you." Nothing else.

And whatever you do, don't sign it.
For a month all was quiet. Then,
coming home early from work
I walked upstairs past people moving furniture

out of her apartment. *No one ever*
wants to get involved, right? a thin white man
in shorts and a t-shirt whispered bitter
behind me. I kept walking

the way Tommy did when he saw me
trying to catch his eye: head down,
gaze nailed to the floor, and then he was gone,
and the questions I wanted to ask him

never became words. That tape
was all I had, till one day,
cleaning house, my mother
held it up:

Do you still want this?

I never play it.

Throw it out then.

So I did.

Dear Yoon

When you went home that night to tell your husband
and he took the swing that missed your jaw
and bruised your arm, I wanted you enough
to see that blue-black Rorschach on your flesh
as a gift. Now, behind me on this train,
a mother worries in your language
that her daughter is too old to find a man.
Ji-in must be sixteen by now, too young
for you to worry yet, and yet the voice
your sister screamed in when she saw my face—
*Go! Be a round-eyed's whore! May your daughter
do the same!*—will not have been forgotten.
Even all these years later your neighbors
will wonder which of them would dare
give their son to such a woman's offspring.

Last night, the small commotion of my spilled drink
turned a woman's face I thought was yours
to where I was sitting. If it had been you,
what would I have said?

Remember the beach in Pusan?
We laughed like newlyweds, took these pictures
I joked our children would someday call treasures.
I'm looking at the one of you on the rock we climbed
to escape the stares that brought back
your talk of suicide. You grabbed my hand,
led me to the edge and we stood gazing out
over the water, a future
waiting for us to cross it.
                              Yoon,
you'll read this only if you read my book.
These lines must end. I have to let you go.

Dear Ji-in

Today in Flushing Meadow Park,
my son perched on my shoulders
singing *Twinkle, twinkle little star*

to what I assume was Venus
in a sky colored the precise
red-and-orange-streaked peach

that hung over Seoul
when your mother turned
on the path circling

Sokchun Lake and cracked her voice
over the words like glass:
I can't bring her. Did she

ever tell you I wanted her to?
When I see you now,
you're still three years old,

riding my shoulders
through Pagoda Park. We traded
hello's and how-are-you's

in sing-song voices
like birds trading the melodies
they recognize each other by,

and then your mother smiled,
and the veil of my foreignness lifted,
and we were the family I imagined.

Surrender

It's in your blood, not yet dangerous
but there, patient, growing. It's in your blood
but I'm out here, sitting powerless

in the middle of my day, pronouncing curse
upon curse against the sickness it can breed
in your blood. It's not yet dangerous,

small enough, they say, that mere watchfulness
will suffice, and they tell me not to be afraid,
but I'm out here, sitting, powerless,

waiting for you to wake, composing this
not to think how much the doctor said
is in your blood and not yet dangerous.

Hindsight renders this moment obvious:
We should have known; we failed; you could be dead.
Out here, we're sitting powerless

as parents always are to take the place
of children pushed too close to the void.
It's in your blood but not yet dangerous.
We're out here, sitting, powerless.

Op Ed

The man who murdered
my wife and son
has been convicted.
If you're reading this,
chances are you know
the prosecutor's argument
for murdering him too,
and I will confess:
when they told me
all he'd done, it was not
in that moment obvious
that justice could be
anything other
than torture slow enough
that the seconds stretched
like days across his pain,
and he was begging for release.

Because all I could hear
in the voices of the officers
who came to tell me
was my wife pleading
with him to let our son
out of the car, and because
the image of her face going slack
as she realized it was no use
punched me to the ground,
and because her voice, from the last
time we argued about it,
came back to me, and I saw her again
hammering each word
with her fist, insisting

she'd be happy
to look a man like him
in the eye and say
as she inched the final blade
all the way in, taking
with his suffering
her own measure
of the lives he took,
that granting him his death
was a waste of mercy—because I knew
I could never do such a thing,
I was sorry she wasn't there.

The trial's punishment phase
begins tomorrow, each side arguing
for the killer's life—his father
and my father among them—as if
his beating heart and breathing lungs
were prizes stacked
above those open-mouthed clowns
with balloons you try to burst
on top of their heads,
at which, just months ago
on the Coney Island boardwalk
my boy and I took aim,
my fingers steadying his
on the water gun's trigger,
trying to win
the big blue teddy bear
in the carny's hand,

and it would be so easy
to stand before the judge,
as some have urged me to do,
and let my wife speak through me.
The jury should know, one friend wrote,

what she would've wanted,
but even a murderer,
even this murderer,
who waited two hours
to end my family's misery
with bullets I've dreamed myself
in front of every night
since the bodies were found,
even he has the right not to die
just because someone else
has decided he must.

Make no mistake: this is not,
as many Christians have told me
it ought to be, about
forgiveness: I do not
forgive him—but no matter
how much I might want him
to die over and over and over again,
I can't at the same time not know
that in the moments after his birth
someone held him
the way I held my son,
and I can't not know
that his eyes, like my son's,
looked out at whoever it was
with nothing in them
but sight and patience,

and I have never been
more scared or more naked:

The infant in my arms
did not yet love me
and maybe never would,
and in that doubt

I understood everything
I had to offer him was nothing
if it didn't stand as proof
that long before the gaze
I was giving back to him,
long before my smile
and the words of welcome
I sang while his mother rested,
long before I felt his first kick
through the skin of her belly,
before she walked into my class
and I thought the rest of my days
would not be long enough
to plumb the depths
of the stare she fixed me with,
long before her father and mine
gathered our new-born bodies
into that same embrace,
with that same fear
and that same hope,
long before any of that,
my love for him
was a collective, human love
he would never
have to work
to deserve.

Sarah's Story

It was, of all the ways we ever touched,
the most intimate: His belly bloomed red,
ragged petals of flesh ringing the void
his small intestines should have filled. I pushed
his insides back inside—they saw, they watched—
carried him to our hospital and prayed.
They followed like blood hounds and when he died
dumped him in a mass grave. That night, I retched
through seven corpses till I recognized
his wounds and lifted him one last time,
properly, into the earth. He was cold,
hard. After I laid him out, I held
his hands to my breasts and whispered his name.
He didn't warm. I kissed him. His eyes stayed closed.

Mirage

A desert has swept itself across my bed,
sun and heat and rippled sand. You are gone.
The only trace of you is in my head.

Beneath you, I was fertile ground planted
with bamboo you harvested again and again.
Then this desert swept itself across my bed,

and cactus grew, green and yellow and red,
marking each spot you touched, and each moan,
the only traces of which are in my head.

I woke this morning thinking you were dead,
a dream explaining why I am alone.
This desert that has swept itself across my bed

feels that permanent. Today, at a parade
you might have liked, I saw in a woman
a trace of you I knew was in my head,

but I knew as well that you were there, solid
in the heat and sun. I turned. You were gone.
A desert has swept itself across my bed.
The only trace of you is in my head.

Your Breasts

Drops of water swelling to let go
of the leaf to which they are clinging—
with my precise deer's tongue,
I lick at them, I try
to drink them in.

After Drought

Knees rooted in the bed on either side
of your belly, my body's a stalk of wheat
bent in summer wind, a bamboo shoot
rising, an orchid, and then all at once a cloud
swelling, a swallow sculpting air, a freed
white dove. You pull me down, but you are hot
beneath me, and the gust that is my own heat
lifts me away: I'm not ready. Outside,
footsteps, voices. Two men. Giggling, we pull
the sheet around us till they pass, but if someone
does see, what will they have seen? A couple
making love. No. More than that: They will
have seen the coming of the rain; they will
have seen us bathe in it, and they will say *Amen.*

Here

Sleeping without you in your bed the night
before I leave, your cat—my friend at last—
cuddled against my feet instead of yours,
I remember our first time three years ago.
After dinner, you passed me the joint.
Looking down, you whispered, *My loins are melting,*
and held my hand tight between your legs.
I drove home the next day for winter break.

Now I will not see your face for a year
or hear your voice, but with your new lover
last night I wrestled to describe the part
of me I call divine. He didn't get it.
Or wouldn't. You smiled patience at me,
and you were right: He'll learn. Or not. We did. Here.

Because

Because I refuse to learn to say goodbye,
these words—but because they are not my skin,
and because my fingers are not syllables,
and because your voice on the phone is not
breath I can take into my mouth and taste,
and the phone when we speak is not your body
in my arms or your hand lifting my chin
so our eyes meet when you say *I love you*,

and because when I imagine your hand
lifting my chin, I want to live within
that moment with you the way language
lives within us, I am here, wrestling these lines
into form, and because the form *is* me
when you read it, I'll be there, and we'll touch.

Now

Heathrow Airport, London. For lunch,
corned beef between two nearly stale slices
of crustless white bread, a jelly donut, juice,
and then a walk through the duty-free shop
looking for the brand of whiskey we drank in Edinburgh.

On the checkout line, smoke rises in front of me
in thin gray spirals from a cigarette
a woman with long pastel-blue nails
rolls slowly between her fingers. I pay,
take a seat near gate twelve

and watch a small boy without shoes
move that magical distance
away from his mother
before he has to turn
to make sure she's still there.

Last night, the bee that ate my face when I was two
came back to interrupt a dream
that made us lovers once again:
A chorus of swallows rose overhead.
You felt it too—we were trespassing—and guided me

back onto the crumbling stone steps
built into the hillside centuries ago
by men you claimed as ancestors. The fort
that once overlooked the island's west coast
was now a church you wanted me to see,

but five women in pink gowns
crowded the entrance. *Bridesmaids*, you whispered,

as if we'd stumbled on a ritual forbidden to us,
and then it was your wedding day,
and just as it happened in real life,

I arrived after you'd spoken your vows,
stood twice at dinner
ready with what I had
to wish you well
and watched your husband twice

lead you away. Then you pulled me
into the lobby of our high school building.
I knew you were asking me to free you,
so I did, but as we turned our backs
on your spouse's bloody corpse

the bee became a lizard
that sunk its teeth into my thigh,
and I bolted upright in my seat, pushing
my face against the window.
I stared down

at the vast expanse
of the Atlantic
and I cried.

I don't know another way to say this:
I'm happier now than we could ever have been.

After The Funeral

That night, again, I dreamed you were leaving,
but this time I was older, and when I walked you
through the marketplace, and you put down
your suitcase to embrace me, I drew
the silence of all the years *you'd* been dead to me
around my right to grief. I wished you gone
and you were. In photographs, I see you
feeding me, your face younger than mine now.
In one, I'm a small bundle on your shoulder,
and the flat of your palm is the world against my back,
teaching me to let go of what is useless. You
have been useless to me. You never knew
the red shepherd I threw my Frisbee for.
In my mind, I matched him stride for stride,
and when he leapt to snatch the floating disc from air,
he called to me and we sailed off, a boy
who could run with wolves, a dog with language
and the gift of flight. I named him Larry,
after you, but true names are secrets,
so I called him Joe.

Between Men

Angry high school kids board the train,
crush the black beret a sleeveless woman drops
past fishnet stockings and stiletto heels.
A bell rings, the door closes, and lights
flash by, and colors, and, at varying
depths, the tunnel opens into caverns filled with
frosted hair and gum-chewed voices. An infant
girl a father holds like cloth he fears to stain
cries the shadow of your eyes into glass.
Grabbing the air in a fist, a voice swings
past my right ear. A face, brown and swollen
and bloody, turns. *Everybody sayin'*
how you gotta be strong, but it's hard *to be strong!*
Nigger fucked me up for talkin' to his wife!
And then it's you and Peter on the platform,
and there is his arm tight around your waist,
and there, the space my empty outstretched hand
defines, and I'm wondering what I need
that I want him to fill it.

After Dancing In The Diana Nightclub
With A Woman My Friend Paid For
Against My Wishes

On the train home, Korean recruits, boys,
holding hands and smiling like lovers,
like the two old men strolling yesterday
among the young couples with children
and the loose circles of teenagers
gathered along the path in Pagoda Park.

I stared the way I'd be ashamed to stare
back home, remembering the night
I let your tongue in my mouth
chase me shivering out into the yard,
and at first I couldn't tell you why,
and then when I was ready, you wouldn't let me.

The men circled five times before they walked
back onto the street, still joined at the palms,
and no one cried out *queer!* or *fag!*
or threw the stones they would've thrown
in most American cities I know.
I followed them till a man in a gray suit

called out *Mi-gook saram!*—an American!—
asking when I stopped to acknowledge him
if I knew Christ. *Yutae-in imnida,*
I answered—I'm Jewish—and he said,
Oh! Sorry, sorry! and hurried away.
The men were gone.

Now, here, alone in my room
with tonight's small celibacy,
I recall how neatly you fit in my lap,
and your hands firm on either side of my face,
and I wish once more for that long moment
when I still had time to turn my head

or to put my fingers over your lips.

After Saying Goodbye To You Three Times In Three Days

At dinner you told me the girl you were
when you believed in God believed herself
a Jedi knight in her lord's army: hidden,
knowing, more powerful than she appeared,
waiting to reveal to those ready to receive it
the light they had to open to or burn,

and the image came to me then that comes
whenever I see street-corner preachers
thumping their Bibles in traffic, or my sweet-faced
born-again students reassure me
I'm in their prayers, or the Jews For Jesus
in the subway tell me it's all about

finding the will to surrender
and be ravished by truth,
the way they say I'm ravished now by greed and lust,
the substitutes we know for love, and so *of course*
I fail to recognize love's absence in my life:
without Christ, how could it be otherwise?

And I cannot help it. The image I carry
away from them of this savior
for whom they are trying to procure me
is of a luminescent phallus
searching for those in whom it can become
a tangible beacon against the nightmare dark

of satan's deceit. I recalled for you
the years of my own belief, striking bargains

with God that just this once—and this once,
and this once, and the once after that—
if he would look the other way, pretend
the darkness in my room or in my mind

shrouded his eyes too, I'd stop whatever-it-was
for good. Long before I met you, I dreamed
a female missionary craved my soul.
Pleading with me to spread who I was wide
to receive the pure voice of her messiah,
she lifted her breasts in her palms and said,

Find nourishment in me! I woke up hard,
the incandescent moon through the trees
casting blue shadows over my bed,
and the way my body moved beneath my hands
had nothing to do with anything I was missing.
Now, on this train out of Manhattan,

we watch the couple in the seat across from us,
her arms wrapped around his back, his head
cradled in the crook of her elbow, mouth
working her nipple through the sheer fabric
you nodded my eyes towards when they boarded.
She lowers her lips to his ear and tastes,

but she's looking at us, smiling a dare
we've been smiling at each other for months.
Another dream: You lay me on the bed
and stroke my face, and your breath—*Don't move!*—
is hot against my cheek. You place
a wreath of kisses around my neck,

suck to the edge of my skin
from collar bone to navel
red florets marking a path

I've carried with me through today
down into this:
my body's reach for you—

and all the times I've wanted
to bend you back across
whatever furniture was there,
and all the times
I've opened hopeful
beneath your gaze and waited—

but this carefully careless brush
of fingers on thighs
is all we allow ourselves,
italics for words we each hope
the other hears as
Take me!

To The Woman At The Bar

Brown hair, leather jacket, torn jeans,
suppose I walk across this room right now
and offer you a drink. Would you tell me

you're a painter, a middle sister with four brothers,
whose mother's work of art is the life
she tries daily to seduce you into? Would you

finger-stir your scotch, eyes averted, waiting
for words you'll know when you hear them
were those you wanted your blond, hovering boyfriend

to say, or leave, or you knew you'd walk out?
And his silence left you no choice?
Would you dance with me, end the evening

on the couch your mother bought wholesale,
pushed against the balcony's grate
so we can fuck overlooking the river?

Instead, will we talk about your work?
Will I leave with your number scribbled
just below my chin in the caricature

you sketch of me as the drummer
I never had the courage to become?
A week from now, will we meet for sushi?

Two nights later, the European art film
with real sex in it? You tell me your name
means pearl in the language your father spoke,

that your mother gave it to you when he left.
You ask me up to see your paintings.
I want to say I see in them

a foreshadowing of what comes next,
but what comes next poses formal problems
I would have to know you to solve.

Ezra's Story

The debate went on for hours: Did Jewish art
require Jewish subjects? And were we bound
as Ghetto artists to be more disciplined
in content, forsaking vision to report
history? That week, a woman's skirt
was found at the Ghetto Gate lined
with smuggled food. She thought quick to "befriend"
the guards, offered them a woman's comfort
and recited the life she claimed as hers—
single with no living relatives—
to keep them from her family. The soldiers,
thank God, accepted, but took as well the loaves
and cans they'd caught her with. She brought me her shame.
I wrote it down, but I've forgotten her name.

Bait And Switch

She steps into my life from cabinets
and closets, where the corners are her home.
This time, she's braved the light with a name
from my past and a warning: He's after her
to give me up. Afraid as much for herself
as for me, she dyes her brown hair blond, finds
an accent she thinks he won't know, and moves us
to a storefront where she gives psychic readings
for five dollars and up. Women and men
crowd in, desperate for hope, willing to pay,
but she'll take only what they can afford.
I bring coffee while she negotiates a price,
then retreat, before the revelations begin,
to the back closet. My home is in the corner.

Home

You come to my room
in the gray sweatshirt
the lover you once asked me
to join you with

left for you to find
the morning he flew
back to Barcelona.

Stretching the sleep
out of your arms,
you let the jersey rise
just enough for me to see

there's nothing underneath
and smile the same smile
you gave that night

when I stood frozen
at the foot of your bed,
watching you lift
the blanket. Yes I saw

he was inside you,
and yes you were both
beautiful, but it was you

singular I wanted,
as I want you now
these last hours
before New York again

becomes my home.
Yesterday, I followed
the narrow streets of your city

past the small café
we sat in my first night here
till I came to the fountain
you said granted you

the childhood wish
you'll never reveal.
I could live here, I thought,

and here you are, and what is waiting
for me beyond the airport is nothing
compared to the red-blond glow
the sun finds in your hair.

With your hands, you show me
where you want me,
and I bend to you,

part with my tongue
these lips that really do
resemble rose petals,
and as if this room, this

house, were suddenly mine
to offer you, I close my arms
around your waist, hold you

tight against this moment
that is not why I came to visit;
and from the night
that two weeks ago

almost ended
where we are right now,
your voice comes back to me,

What would you change?
And my answer,
I'd want not to be afraid,
but I realize I am afraid:

I *could* live here.
You push me back
onto the bed,

turn the clock
to the wall
and whisper
Stay!

Yossi's Story

When he was two I had to stuff a piece
of cloth in his mouth till he almost died
so he would understand it wasn't hide-
and-seek we were playing with the Nazis.
First he laughed, then he cried, and when his face
turned blue, I let him breathe. He understood.
Noise from three floors up saved us that night, led
the soldiers to our store of food. This place
is all I have left of him. I used to come
once a month and cry for the wasted time
the years of raising him became the day
Arabs shot him in Jerusalem. We saved
the lives our parents gave us, and we lived
to see a Jewish state. That's all I'll say.

What There Is For Me
To Hold To

I.

You talked about your brother like a stranger.
My father trains his eyes on my silence,
lifts his drink to his mouth and sips. I do
the same. My brother *was* a stranger, except

he knew my name, and where I lived, and where—
when he let his friends in to rob our home—
the big and small treasures of my young life
could be uncovered. He helped them carve

"kike" a half-inch deep into my door,
and they pulled my shelves off the wall,
trampled my books, and even now I can conjure
the sneer his lips must have curled into

while they worked. The last time
I saw him alive he was nineteen, sitting
in the kitchen with the girlfriend who didn't die
when the car the drunk was driving opened

against a tree, and my brother's neck broke
in the tall grass lining the Taconic Parkway.
My father puts his drink down.
I know I could've been around more

back then, he says, and I'm fourteen, riding
in his car on the way to what should have been
my brother's thirteenth birthday party. Beneath
the overpass that means we're halfway

to Brooklyn, my father puts his hand on my knee,
and against an accusation from somewhere
other than between us, he defends himself:
I should have been around more, I know,

but we're all responsible for this—this:
my brother arrested for mugging
an old woman not far from here
on Union Turnpike—*we're all*
responsible: your mother, me, even you.

2.

I stood between them whose faces my face
repeats, between the dead and the living,
myself alive and dying, and the rabbi
spoke of friendship and reconciliation,
and the twins cried, and all four grandparents
sobbed, and my mother stood in the calcified
silence of her own anger, and all I
could think was how my brother's death
had left the empty spaces between us empty;
and they lowered the coffin into the ground,
and we shoveled the customary shovelfuls of dirt,
and before he drove off, my father held me
like a branch he didn't want to fall from,
and then the wind carried him away.

Now, here, facing this granite
that's all of my brother
I've left to face, I remember driving
past Florida, NY to the bar-mitzvah
of my dead uncle's son. *The last time*
your brother ran away, my mother said,
and the cops called for me to take him home,
I wondered how he got so far south so damned fast.

He was here. She shrugged the same bitter grin
Ramiel later gave when I stood for the aliyah
his father should have been there to say.
The week's portion was Lekh Lekha,
God's command to Abraham
to go. In my family,
the men also leave.
Or they die. I will no longer
prepare to be next.

Kashrut

A table is an altar.
—*The Talmud*

I sit with knife and fork to eat this remnant
of a life. Days ago, on the block this bird
was born for, with a blade sharp and faultless,
a butcher did his job, and a creature
of the living God became food. The lungs
were searched for blemish, the other organs checked,
that nothing of this world that passed
through this body I'm passing through mine
stayed long enough to become a sickness.

Then the butcher covered with earth the life
pooled at his feet, recited the blessing
that returns to the ground what the ground
at God's word gave forth and, with salt to draw
the rest of the blood, began to render death
fit and ready for human consumption.

Melissa's Story

The doctor gave instructions like a spy:
Be there, seven pm, on the dot.
If you're not, I'm gone. Don't even think about
another appointment. Got it? That day,
of course, there was traffic, and the money
had to be in small, old bills. *You will get*
in my car as if we were lovers. At the spot,
you'll step out first. Walk when and where I say
Make a mistake and I leave. Understood?
I did. Somehow it went without a snag,
and there I was, legs open on a bed,
with a man crouched between them like a dog.

He reached into me and scraped away the life
I'd almost made, not yet mine to give.

Commerce

Blond in light rain, no umbrella: *Y'need*
a date, mister? she smiles. I shake my head.

Y'sure? Blow job? Hand job? I live right down
the block . . . and I don't feel exactly when

the dense knot of rage tightens my gut
into the grin I give back, but I watch the bright

red-lipsticked invitation on her face
as she passes—her teeth so precise,

she has to be expensive—and I hate her
the way I hated the call last night at dinner

offering a sample package of baby formula
tucked into a free issue of *Parenting* magazine

with *the chance to enjoy exclusive discounts*
on many other infant care products

because market experts have foreseen a child
we don't yet even know we want.

The assumption that all I do is want.
Then the old man's voice, *But don't you want*

me to love you? I trembled naked
beneath his hands, ran, when he lifted

them, into silence and sex, ignorance
and safety, and the droplets dance

off her bleached mane as she walks by, tossing
in a kiss the offer I refuse to another man

who catches it and puts it in his pocket,
but he too says no—or so I assume,

because she keeps going, crossing the street
in high-heeled steps he doesn't bother watching,

that I do, until the crowd on this uptown avenue
closes behind her, and I'm standing nude

in my high-school-first-time fantasy: I let
the mower idle in the musk of fresh cut grass,

and the girl who had this prostitute's hair,
and her friend, and *Spare some change, guy?*—

a man's voice from beneath a beard
like a forest's undergrowth. I jingle

my pocket and drop into his cupped palm
the coins I have. *Good luck*, I tell him,

eyes focused on the air just above his head,
half of me still beneath the girls' mouths,

but he grips my hand, grins missing teeth,
and so I'm reaching for more, doing the math

to pay his way into a shower, a shave,
maybe a massage, some small reprieve

from the street's dirt and daily hostilities.
And the woman whose books tally the men

who've left themselves in or on her,
what would her reprieve be? In the tight

ball of my fist, cash he hurries away from
without knowing it's there. In her bedroom,

a man who's given what she thinks she's worth
standing while she unzips his pants, and my mouth

tastes what she tastes, and I'm twelve,
sitting on the stoop with my friends.

The old man stares between my parted knees,
reminds me I said I'd help him carry his bags

upstairs. *I'll pay you. I've got weak legs.*
He waits, daring me to call him the liar

he is, but I don't. Can't. Won't. *A dollar?*
I sit still. The other boys' eyes widen

as he pulls a wad of bills from his green
windbreaker. *No, two,* he says, peels them off,

and I do not know how not to take them.

Bill's Story

He talked about her like she was a boat.
You just loaded the ship, son. Where the wind
takes it is out of your hands, hear? She'll find
a port to dock in. Just be glad you got
what you wanted without getting shot.
Her parents were no better, as if I'd planned
to make her pregnant. We begged them not to send
her away. Once she was gone, they moved out.

Not long after the birth-month, her single
letter came: *I named him Bill. Then they took him.*
Years later, I drove to where the postmark
pointed. No one would speak to me. I still
hope, though. My son is old enough to look,
and I deserve to tell him who I am.

The Silence Of Men

A man I've never dreamed before walks
into my apartment and sits in the green
chair where I do my writing. He carries
in his left hand a large erect penis
which he places silently on the floor.
The phallus begins to waltz to music
I cannot hear, its scrotum a skirt;
its testicles, legs cut off at the knees.

I want to know why this disfigured
manhood has been brought to me. I look up,
but my guest is gone. His organ, deflating
in short spasms like an old man coughing,
spreads itself in a pool of shallow blood.
The silence between us is the silence of men.

The Speed And Weight Of Justice

You and I left this unfinished business
unfinished for too long, and now it's late.
Your flight leaves in two days. Tomorrow,

I have a date to help an old friend replace
china his ex-fiancée shattered against the wall
in their worst fight, which I witnessed. I'm

his lift to the warehouse, and then he
and his new girlfriend will join me
and my wife at our house for dinner.

You're smiling: Narrative always leads us away
from what our bodies lean towards.
I want you, I say. You whisper, *Where can we go?*

and it's so much more touch than words
that I carry the sounds with me on the train
the way I would've carried the texture

of your nipples on my palms. A man
parades in fatigues muttering *Kill
the bastards!*, pronouncing

each passenger *Dangerous!*
who dares to meet his gaze. I retreat
to where your question takes me:

The scene plays, my flesh rises, and the distance
this ride is putting between us vanishes
till the bell rings, the doors whoosh open

and I walk out squinting in sunlight
onto the streets of my marriage.
At the corner, the slow noise

of afternoon lovemaking delights
a herd of teenagers who call to the window,
urging the lovers to show themselves.

Across the street, a pale woman
holds tight to her shirtless lover,
oblivious to the hard lock his eyes have

on the ass of a teenage boy,
whose blond hair hangs wet
to the small of his back. Behind them,

in the crowd of weekend shoppers searching
for the bargains Jackson Heights is known for,
another woman, her hejab coming loose,

two bags balanced in one arm, chases
a girl dressed in yellow and white, whose head
the woman's shouting finally turns. The child's face,

scarred across the left cheek from jawbone
to upper lip, conjures for me the acid
they said last night on TV seared the skin

in which another daughter refused the man
her father chose for her; and the twelve-year-old bride
my student wrote about: taken

from her home in Spain to Afghanistan
and—a single letter making it almost
comic—*penetrated anually...She couldn't*

leave her bed for three days. And in today's mail:
a son too young yet to know he has a mother
will lose her: he has no legal father.

And they have already gathered the stones,
chosen with care not to cause too much damage
too soon, and dug the hole in which they'll kill her,

and when the last rock shatters her last thought
they will call it justice, and so to ask—
as I've been wanting to do these past weeks—

where the justice is in our having met
now, when our separate lives separate us,
or, rather, we allow them to, so much

more effectively than the veils these women wore
protected them—to ask this is to ask precisely what?
I stand at my front door, the key still in my pocket,

and re-enter the room we never gave ourselves
the chance to find. Maybe someday we will,
but what would be different? I'd still arrive

here, home, in love; still feel myself there,
with you, coaxing, being coaxed into presence,
until presence is all we know, and shadows

are what we are of the complex beings
we believe ourselves to be: the people
we need always to come back to.

Story

In the Talmud, they imagine a man fixing his roof.
A sudden storm looms in the west. The building wind
wraps the white hem of his robe tight around his legs,
just like the cloth the fruit seller down the block
uses to protect a woman's apples
from bruising. She puts them in her basket,
glances over her shoulder at the gathered
darkness moving towards her like a wall,
and runwalks home at just the right speed
to bring her to the spot on the sidewalk
where, when the squall's fist
punches the man into midair,
his trajectory will end.

The rabbis were concerned with damage—
whom to hold accountable for what—
and so they imagined this as well: Just
before the man's descent begins, or maybe
it's just before the woman's body
breaks his fall, his penis rises,
her dress billows up
and her legs open, and because
she too is naked underneath her clothes,
he slips into her, ejaculating
on impact. Not rape,
the wise ones all agree, though all agree
real damage has been done, the question is—
and I will leave them to it—how much
and why the woman is entitled to collect.

I'm thinking this is a love story.
For years the man has watched the woman walk

twice a week from the market to her home,
and even in winter his gaze is a warm breeze
against her skin. You know the tale:
forbidden to each other
by parents of different tribes,
married off as soon as possible
into lives course-corrected and unhappy,
their eyes are all they have to love with.

So he's up on the roof, this time's excuse
to see her saunter by, and when she does,
he unbalances himself
to glimpse her breasts. The gust,
as it sweeps him onto her,
enters him, and I've planted
a hedge for them to fall behind, a gift,
like the weather is a gift,
and they take their time,
for surely heaven wanted it that way.

The Talmud Says

A snake is an evil. A woman
who sees one and doubts
if he desires her, let her remove
her clothing in his presence.
If he coils in among her garments
he lusts. If not, not.

A snake is an evil. A woman
who knows there is one
that does indeed lust for her,
let her contrive a time and a place
that he might see her in congress
with her husband.

A snake is an evil. A woman
who fears the sight of her
and her husband may inflame
the serpent's desire, let her
throw at him some locks of hair
and the words *I am impure!*

And if, God forbid, the snake
has already penetrated, the woman
should seat herself on two barrels
with her thighs parted. Beneath her
let fat meat be thrown on burning coals,
and a bowl of cress
soaked in sweet smelling wine
placed beside the fire. Hold in readiness
a pair of tongs. Wait. The serpent
will leave her for the smell of the food.
When he is caught, against his return, burn him.

Isaac's Story

The woman's swelling body looked misplaced
in the midst of all they did to murder us.
This embryo must perish, der Hauptmann's voice
prescribed the quick removal of a cyst.
If not, we'll take it at birth. He smiled the rest,
flicked his wrist to let the woman pass.
Two months later, the boy was born. The bris—
with our mohel dead, the doctor did his best
to learn the prayers—took place the night
they hanged a man for smuggling and shot
his wife and kids for being who they were.
I held the baby in my lap, but before
the child lost his flesh as we'd been taught,
we whispered kaddish: the dead were there.

You Will, Of Course, Assume It Is For You

I wake to this hardness without desire.

Drumbeat.
Rhythm.
Heartbeat.
Sorrow.

Blood-pulse passed from man to man like breath.

Yesterday, the mohel took, sharp
and sterile from his bag, the clamp and blade,
asked those of us crowded into the room
for the cutting from a boy
of the skin he was born with
for quiet.

The wine-soaked cloth against the baby's mouth,
the silence that we all knew what was coming,
metal meeting metal, and the shield
held in its grandfather's lap
screamed

as I and my father
and his father
and all the men in this house
and their fathers
screamed

as our sons not yet born
and all the sons will scream

who wait to follow them

as Abraham screamed
who, because he heard
the word of God,
did it to himself.

My Father Loses His Grip

You can pee in the ocean but not in the pool.
Waves are bigger than I can hold my breath.
Out there, a boat in a bathtub, the fourth
one today. The water's fingers pull
my father's arms apart. Be careful:
The sun bakes little boys. Salt in my mouth,
sand in my swimsuit. Do fish have teeth?
I'm waiting for God to wrap me in a towel
and carry me to heaven. I'm tumbled,
grab rocks that don't grab back, gulp air:
My lungs are too small to float. Above my voice,
I know I can't be seen. I hear my name crumbled
and the water parts. Hands and my father's face
descend, lift me to his eyes, wrap me in his fear.

Covenant

I.

Your dreams these days wake you crying
into words we puzzle over,
trying like street-corner psychics
to read back from what you know how to say
to the precise image you couldn't sleep through:
noon daugheh, "hot bread" in your mother's tongue,
or apple juice, or
toop bauzi, "play ball."

Just months ago, when your butt still fit neatly
in my palm, I calmed your crying with song.
Now you want the thing itself—apple juice,
bread, ball—as if seeking confirmation
that the roots of your thoughts
dig hard into substance,
and when you hold in your hand the object
you need to know you didn't just imagine—
last night it was your stuffed Kermit—
you let us lay you down,
and you sleep again.

Not me, rocking
here for hours

in this chair
my mother rocked me in

when I was your size.
I've been watching

Manhattan's skyline
emerge from morning mist,

weary travelers
met by chance

on a country road.
My own wanderlust,

barely sated,
pushes hard

for me to join
them, but I've made

promises, not the ones
you'll think, though they

count too, no,
deeper oaths

that crush your life
if you break them,

the way I thought
when I was a boy

the god of Abraham
would crush me

for what I'd learned
my mouth could hold.

2.

A long hallway and a door,
and white moths cover the ceiling and the walls,

and the one I have to find, the purple one,
flies through to the other side
where I'm kneeling, naked, a child
in my adult flesh, crying,
frozen to the spot
by words a voice
chants, *If you remember*
you'll go crazy, and then my hands are tied
behind my back, and he stands over me,
fists clenched, screaming, and I repeat after him,
also screaming, *If I remember I will go crazy!*

That dream stopped
the year your mother
entered my life,

but last night
after you slept,
I saw him again.

This time I faced him,
and I knew him,
and a boy's rage

rose within me,
and I got up
off my knees,

and the ropes fell
from my hands,
and I towered

above him, and he
prostrated himself,
and when I spoke

I pictured him
as Abraham:

           Your bastard sex
will burn and wither at another's touch,
and the permanent fear of someone knowing that
will make your heart a rat-infested pit,
and keep you begging at humanity's crotch,
taking for love what drips through the cracks.

The Haunting

My belly grows with every pound I gain,
accumulates like snow on a small hill.
My lover spreads her hands across the swell,
Does this child have a name? The grin
she offers, talisman to dull the pain
her words are not intended to instill,
wounds her face, cracks it like a shell.
Boy or girl? If you had to choose, which one?

I force myself to answer, laugh to hide
the half-acknowledged fear her questions wake:
bodies rising decomposed from earth,
calling to their bones the skin of youth,
fucking, giving birth, then falling back:
their graves wombs; my life their marriage bed.

Worst Nightmare

To my right an Asian woman reads aloud
from a book I can't see, in a language
I could ask her about, but she closes it,

slings her backpack over one shoulder
and calling *Bye!* to the people behind
the bar, runs smack into the gray-haired

street-cleaner, whose green hat with his broom
flies into the gutter, where a car blasting
reggae out to the world stops just in time.

He looks to scream at her, but she's gone,
so he walks into the pub, orders
a beer to calm himself and turns to me,

Fucking chinks, send 'em back where they came from!
I stop writing, look up into a stare
daring me to disapprove, and then a voice

behind me adds, *Yeah, the chinks and the niggers!*
and someone else calls out *spics and queers!*
then *japs and gooks!* and as a chorus fills the room

with whom we'd be better off without,
the men finger my clothing, pick
at my skin and hair, looking for a sign

that I belong; and their words keep coming,
rising like red welts from the skin of their lives:
lesbian cunts, dot-heads, camel-jockeys.

The bartender puts a check in the no box
next to each epithet on the chart, but I see
kike isn't too far down the list, so I reach for the knife

on the next table, ready to kill if I have to,
except my left hand is suddenly bound
with tefilin, and my shoulders are wrapped in a tallis

that makes it difficult to move. I see in the mirror
above the jukebox shoulder-length peyos
dangling from my ears, a salt-and-pepper beard

descending below my neck: I have become
the rabbi who in eighth grade tried
to persuade me my home was with Torah,

not my family. My wife, as the woman
whose rush to get where she was going
started all this trouble, enters the dream

with our naked son in her arms. Seeing
he's not circumcised, the mob steps back.
If that's his kid, one of them says, *he can't be Jewish.*

Ashamed to have doubted me, they turn away,
all but one wizened old man
who buys me a Bloody Mary, lifts

his straight-up double scotch to his lips,
smiles like he's found Jesus
and, with a whispered *L'chaim!,* disappears.

Jill's Story

The last one to rape me
whispered "Jewish whore"
with each thrust,
and his friends chanted
"train–train–train–train."
That's what they called me
in the hall between classes.
Even the cute new
math teacher said,
"Hello Train" every morning,
till someone must've told him
what it meant.

She glanced at my face, read there
I-don't-know-what, but I think
to spare me having to find
the right thing to say,
she changed the subject.
You have a girlfriend?

Yes.

She Jewish?

No.

Jill pushed me away.
So, you're just like all the others.
Turn from your own people
for some shikseh's cunt!

I didn't go after her
when she walked out, but I did

remember the dream: They placed
the chair they'd chained me to
at the head of the table,
lashed my hands to the hands
of the woman roped belly down
on top of it, and each one
who climbed onto her
kissed me first, saying,
You know what this is for.

When I woke up
only her eyes were with me,
open and unblinking and tearless,
as mine could never have been.

Ethics Of The Fathers

Moses received the Torah from Sinai
and passed it on to Joshua, who gave
it in his turn to The Elders, and love
or duty, or maybe both, explain why
we still hand it down, even if we die
doing so. The Church burned us alive,
the Romans did worse...but you who give
yourselves to goyishe women, you lie
with their gods as well, and so we cast you out.
The rabbi paused, whispered *Come back*, and left
the stage. No applause. Behind me, a man laughed.
Beside me, a woman squirmed in her seat.

In love, my love, I've given myself to you,
neither god nor goddess, and not a Jew.

Catching My Breath

My body has learned many lies,
but here, in this bed we share,
they fall from me till I am clean,
a tree in winter,
awaiting the new season.

Poem From The Barnes
and Noble Café

I.

When I started walking
    I wasn't counting steps.
        I was thinking how these days

were not what I'd hoped
    life would reduce me to,
        but when I crossed the street,

the switch that throws itself
    inside my brain
        whenever I walk alone

threw itself, and I was mouthing
    numbers, tallying each stride
        as if I were building meaning.

Then I was here, in the bookstore,
    looking for that volume
        on Iranian cinema, which I found

more easily than I thought I would,
    so I rode the escalator
        down to Music—a whim;

I haven't bought a CD
    in months—and almost knocked
        an olive-skinned man

with a black and white keffiyeh
   wrapped around his neck
      into Britney Spears' nearly naked

cardboard flesh. I grabbed his arm
   to steady him; he gripped me back,
      and someone slowing down to watch

might've thought we were old friends.
   He continued on. I turned, stared
      at the fringed fabric hanging down

the brown leather of his jacket—
   so much like a tallis, I thought—
      and recalled my own keffiyeh,

bought twenty years ago,
   after Sabra and Shatila, from a
      Black man with French-tinged English.

A shill for the Arabs,
   my grandmother bit into air
      I know she wished was him

when she saw it. I wish
   the keffiyeh had meant
      solidarity, or sympathy, or anything

better than escape, but it was
   an escape, and wearing it
      was a kind of freedom,

as there is freedom in wandering
   these aisles, putting aside
      Tangerine Dream for Axiom of Choice,

for a blues compilation we could dance to,
　　or for the Klezmatics, whose music
　　　　on the sound system also

invites dance, and so I'm dancing
　　a small shuffle into Show Tunes,
　　　　remembering Surprise Lake Camp's

Fiddler On The Roof, the boy
　　who played Tevye, fat and athletic,
　　　　and when he danced, his belly

bounced out from under
　　his white shirt, and his tzitzis twirled
　　　　in the red stage lighting

like poorly placed stripper's tassels,
　　and we all clapped, laughing,
　　　　singing along, hoping

it would never end. I moved him
　　the way I move myself, step-by-step
　　　　through the choreography,

keeping time with a chord
　　on the grand piano
　　　　that echoes in me still

as I bring the songs I want
　　to the cash register. I sign for them
　　　　as I've signed for so much else in my life

and take the escalator up three flights
　　for a cup of mint tea. Turning
　　　　from the counter, I catch

in the corner of my eye
        the keffiyeh from downstairs
                opening to a square, folding

to a triangle, and the man
        I bumped into smiles at me,
                nods at the chairs he and his friends

are getting up from, drapes
        the cloth around his neck,
                and leaves. On his table,

The New York Times: priests
        using children for sex,
                and George W. Bush wants

money to promote marriage
        and to fight a war he says
                will rid us of our fears.

I'm thinking how much
        the world needs fear right now,
                to step back from the mouth

of what has not yet happened,
        like you'd want a suicide bomber to do,
                or a soldier with orders to shoot civilians.

When you and I danced at our wedding,
        arms raised, hands tracing
                Persian rhythms in the air,

and when they lifted us on chairs
        and danced the hora, your family
                and mine, whatever we erased

it was not difference,
    and so music is an answer
        to the question I'm trying to ask,

for it is nothing when we come together
    if it is not rhythm and melody,
        counterpoint and harmony,

and you push yourself against my mouth,
    and I'm kissing every year you've lived,
        each thousand years of your country's history,

the centuries of Islam, carpets
    woven, children
        nursed, harvests

lost to the weather, the will
    of God, all of it
        vibrating live beneath your skin,

and you guide me, with your own hand
    take me to the spot
        where fear and hope, pain

and joy, merge to become
    the irreducible fact of your flesh,
        and it's like when the band reaches

the last beat, and the dancers
    hang suspended
        in the final resolution:

It *is* peace, and if they, if we,
    could stay there, there would be peace.

2.

I remember Joe taking Patty and me one night to Jones Beach. *Don't try to swim,* he warned. *The undertow will drag you out.* We walked in up to our ankles. Patty started dancing, kicking her legs up in a clumsy can-can, splashing me till my shirt was soaked through. When we got home, we slept in the same bed.

After the murder—Rose, Patty's mother, was found stuffed in a hall closet, stabbed sixteen times with a serrated knife; Joe was the only suspect, but there wasn't enough evidence to prosecute—after the murder, I kept to myself, huddled with friends Patty didn't know. When she came to tell me she was leaving to live with her aunt in New Jersey, I stood away from her, a monosyllabic *Bye!* my only answer.

When Joe came a few weeks later to collect his stuff, the woman from next door hid in our hall closet, the one where the termites had swarmed earlier in the year. She knew, she said, *things* she was afraid to tell the cops.

That was also the year Sandy got sick for the last time, and she knew she was going to die, had refused to be my girlfriend because of it. I didn't go see her, never, that I remember, worried she might want to see me—and then she died.

I'm not being hard on myself.

I know I was only thirteen, and love at that age denies dying, but now I'm forty, and the little boy

who calls me Richard instead of Dad could die tomor-
row. As could you. As many will, even perhaps the man
with the keffiyeh, in whose paper I read another headline:
three youths, Arabs, arrested in France for bombing a syn-
agogue I could've been in, and of course Israel should pull
out now, and of course Palestine's independence should
be declared this moment,

the earth transformed to a tent where we all break bread,
each of us carrying what we've seen
the way musicians carry music
in the moments before they start playing.

Notes

Who Knew: "Kaddish" is the memorial prayer Jews say for the dead.

Slice of Life: "Pyong" is a unit of measurement in Korea that is roughly equivalent to 3.954 square yards. "Chamshil" is a part of Seoul.

Ibrahim's Story: "Erev Shabbat" is Friday night; the phrase means, literally, Sabbath evening.

What There Is For Me To Hold To: An aliyah is when someone, traditionally a man, comes up to say the blessing over the reading of the Torah. It is considered an honor. "Lekh Lekha" are the first two words in Hebrew of the command God gives to Abram in Genesis 12:1, "The Lord said unto Abram: 'Go forth from your native land and from your father's house to the land that I will show you.'"

Kashrut: The title of this poem is the nominal form of the word kosher; it is also the word used to refer to the entire body of Jewish dietary law. The lines "...the blessing/that returns to the ground what the ground/at God's word gave forth..." refer to the practice of "kisooey hadam" or "covering the blood," which the ritual slaughterer does by covering the blood of a just-killed animal with dirt.

The Talmud Says: In their book, *Hebrew Myths*, Robert Graves and Raphael Patai note the fact that, during the time of the Talmud, there was a popular belief that snakes desired intercourse with women. This poem is based on the solutions Graves and Patai record the rabbis of the Talmud as having prescribed.

Isaac's Story: "Bris" is the Yiddish word for circumcision; a "mohel" is a man specially trained to perform circumcisions; "kaddish" is the Jewish prayer for the dead. In *The Kovno Ghetto Diary*, Avraham Tory records the fact that the Gestapo made pregnancy in the ghetto illegal and ordered that every pregnancy had to be terminated.

You Will, Of Course, Assume It Is For You: The custom at Jewish circumcisions is to use a piece of cloth to place a few drops of wine, supposedly to dull the pain of the operation, on the lips of the boy who is about to be cut. The man who holds the boy in his lap when the cutting is done is called the "sandek." To be chosen to be the sandek at a circumcision ceremony is a great honor.

Worst Nightmare: "Tefilin" are the phylacteries that observant Jewish men wear when they say their morning prayers Sunday through Friday; "peyos" are the earlocks worn by Hasidic men; "l'chaim" is a Jewish toast meaning, in Hebrew, "to life."

Covenant: "Noon daugheh" and "Toop bauzi" are transliterations of Persian.

Ethics Of The Fathers: The first three lines of this poem are a direct quote from the beginning of the book of the Talmud that, in English, is called Ethics (or sometimes Chapters) Of The Fathers. "Goyim" is the word, sometimes used pejoratively, for non-Jews; "goyishe" is the adjectival form. The word itself is not pejorative; literally it means "nations."

Poem From The Barnes and Noble Café: A tallis is a Jewish prayer shawl. Tzitzis are the ritually tied fringes hanging from each of the four corners. Orthodox Jewish men wear a small tallis with tzitzis as an undergarment. It is this undergarment that is referred to in the lines about the tzitzis of the boy who played Tevye.

Previously Published CavanKerry New Voices

Howard Levy, *A Day This Lit*

Karen Chase, *Kazimierz Square*

Peggy Penn, *So Close*

Sondra Gash, *Silk Elegy*

Sherry Fairchok, *Palace of Ashes*

Elizabeth Hutner, *Life with Sam*

Joan Cusack Handler, *GlOrious*

Eloise Bruce, *Rattle*

Celia Bland, *Soft Box*

Catherine Doty, *Momentum*

Georgianna Orsini, *Imperfect Lover*

Christopher Matthews, *Eye Level, 50 Histories*

Joan Seliger Sidney, *Body of Diminishing Motion*

Christian Barter, *The Singers I Prefer*

Laurie Lamon, *The Fork Without Hunger*

Robert Seder, *To the Marrow*

Andrea Carter Brown, *The Disheveled Bed*

Our Mission

Through publishing and programming, CavanKerry Press connects communities of writers with communities of readers. We publish poetry that reaches from the page to include the reader, by the finest new and established contemporary writers. Our programming brings our books and our poets to people where they live, cultivating new audiences and nourishing established ones.